TO SARAH
BAPTISM DAY
THE

WHEN
STARS
COME OUT

TO EILEEN

who opened the door

WHEN STARS COME OUT

Bedtime Psalms for Little Ones

BY L. J. SATTGAST
ILLUSTRATIONS BY NANCY MUNGER

WHEN STARS COME OUT

published by Gold'n'Honey Books
a part of the Questar publishing family

International Standard Book Number: 0-88070-641-4

Printed in Hong Kong

For information:
Questar Publishers, Inc.
Post Office Box 1720
Sisters, Oregon 97759

95 96 97 98 99 00 01 — 10 9 8 7 6 5 4 3 2

Contents

Foreword

Lovely books for little children are so important.
If these young ones can gain an early love
of being read to, and then a love of reading
for themselves, their lives
will be enriched.

And certainly a beautiful book with Psalms
put to rhyme will stick in their minds year after year, as
Mother Goose has stayed in ours!

Linda Sattgast has done a superb work.

RUTH BELL GRAHAM

The Songs of David

A little boy named David
lived in Israel many years ago.
He was called a shepherd because he took care
of his father's sheep.

David loved God with all his heart.
While he was out in the field watching the sheep,
he played a harp and sang songs about God.

God loved David, too.
When David grew up, God chose him
to be the king of Israel.

David wrote songs all his life.
Many of those songs are in the Bible,
in the Book of Psalms.
So sometimes David is called
"the sweet psalmist of Israel."

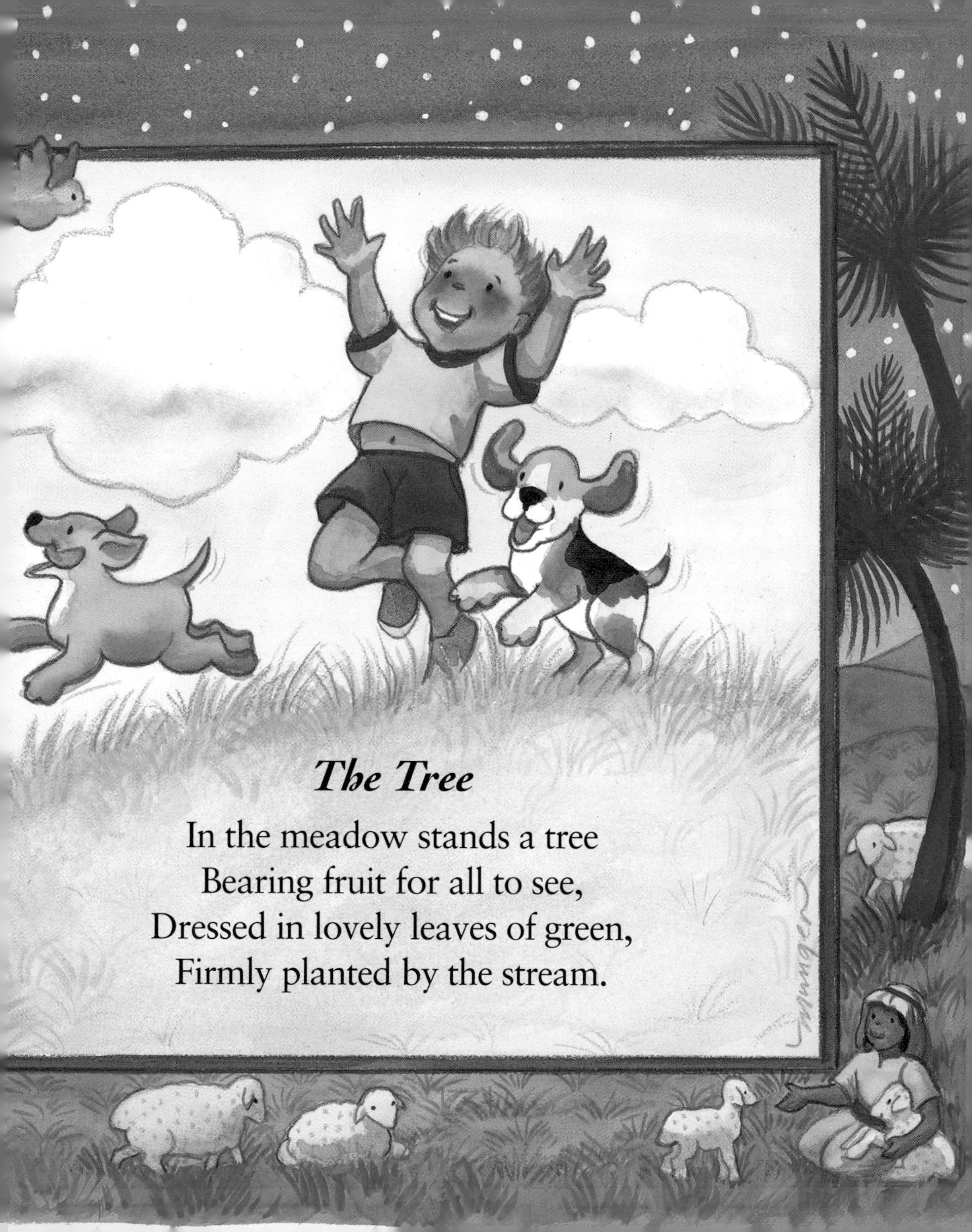

The Tree

In the meadow stands a tree
Bearing fruit for all to see,
Dressed in lovely leaves of green,
Firmly planted by the stream.

Branches reaching to the sky
Whisper as the wind goes by—
"If you love God's Word, *you'll* be
As strong and lovely as a tree."

Blessed is the man who does not walk
in the counsel of the wicked
or stand in the way of sinners
or sit in the seat of mockers.
But his delight is in the law of the Lord,
and on his law he meditates day and night.
He is like a tree planted by streams of water,
which yield its fruit in season
and whose leaf does not wither.
Whatever he does prospers.

PSALM 1:1-3

Silver and Gold

Silver and gold,
Silver and gold,
What could be better
Than silver and gold?

BIBLE

The law from your mouth is more precious to me than

All of the stories
That I have been told—
The Bible is better
Than silver and gold.

thousands of pieces of silver and gold. —*Psalm 119:72*

Pathfinder

Just a little beam of light
        Shining bright,
        In the night,
Keeps my feet upon the path
And helps me find the way.

Your word is a lamp to my feet

and a light for my path. —Psalm 119:105

If I take a little look
In the Book,
God's Holy Book,
I will learn to do what's right
And follow God each day.

BIBLE

The Sun

The sun pokes his head
Up over the hill
And looks around.

Then he jumps
Into the sky
Laughing,
Prancing,
Leaping,
Dancing,
Racing to be—

The first one into bed!

In the heavens he has pitched
a tent for the sun,
which is like…a champion
rejoicing to run his course.
It rises at one end of the heavens
and makes its circuit to the other…

PSALM 19:4–6

Shhhhhh

All day I've
Frolicked and
Played and
Jostled and
Jumped and...

Giggled and
Laughed and
Hollered and
Made such a riot—

But now it's time to be…

Quiet.

Be still and know that I am God. —Psalm 46:10

Still and Quiet

Still and quiet is the night,
Not a fear alarms.
Still and quiet now am I
In my mother's arms.

I have stilled and quieted my soul;

like a weaned child with its mother...

O Israel, put your hope in the Lord
both now and forevermore. —*Psalm 131:2-3*

Not to worry, not to fret,
Even though I'm small.
God is up in heaven
Watching over all.

Song in the Night

When, one by one,
The stars come out
And darkness gathers
All about…

By day the Lord directs his love, at night his song is with me—a prayer to the God of my life. —*Psalm 42:8*

I hear God singing
Quietly,
"I love you—
And you love Me."

The Moon

O, the moon,
        The moon,
                The moon,
Shining like a silver spoon,
Watches twinkling stars go by
As he sails across the sky.

God made the great lights—the sun to govern the day...the moon and stars

O, the moon,
The moon,
The moon,
Smiling down into my room,
Yellow sun is bold and bright—
But silver moon will rule the night.

to govern the night. —Psalm 136:7-8

Hush, Little One

I went to bed and said good night,
        But I woke up in such a fright—
Mommy, please turn on the light!
        Hush, little one, it'll be all right.

He who watches over you

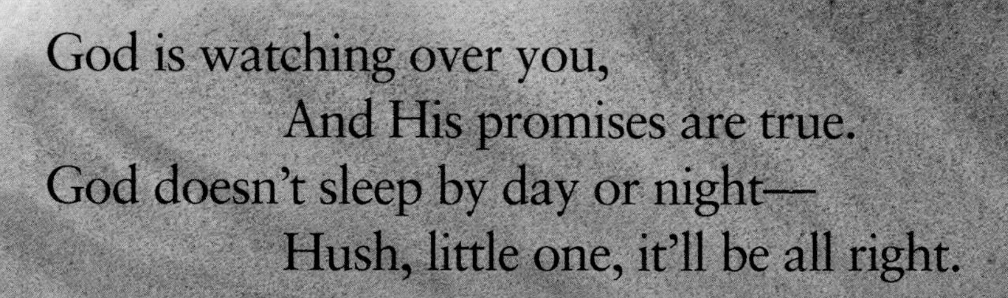

God is watching over you,
And His promises are true.
God doesn't sleep by day or night—
Hush, little one, it'll be all right.

will not slumber; indeed, he who watches over Israel will neither slumber nor sleep. —Psalm 121:3-4

My Shepherd

If God is my Shepherd
    And I am His sheep,
I know that He's with me
    Whenever I sleep.

Bible

I'll wake in the morning
So happy to know
That God will be with me
Wherever I go.

The Lord is my shepherd,
I shall lack nothing.

PSALM 23:1

Your Choice

Whenever you feel like a grump,
And look like you're down in the dump,
Oh, how I dread
When you get out of bed
And go moping about like a frump.

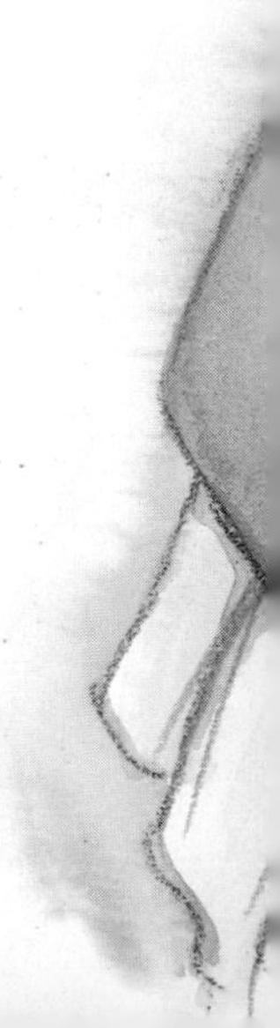

This is the day the Lord has made;
let us rejoice and be glad in it. —Psalm 118:24

But when you can wake up and say,
My, what a wonderful day!
It's hard to be sad,
You'll surely be glad
For God is who made it that way!

Wonderfully Made

First one circle… then another,
Then some arms and legs and toes,
Draw a smile and two round eyes
And in the middle put the nose.
Don't forget the belly button—
Is that all? Now let me see…

Hmmmm…

Although this is a lovely picture,
I'm sure glad that *God* made *me*!

I praise you because I am fearfully and wonderfully made. —Psalm 139:14

If you, O Lord, kept a record of sins,
O Lord, who could stand?

Here I Sit

Here I sit
In a corner
With my little dolly.
I'm so glad
God loves me
Even when I'm naughty.

But with you there is forgiveness... —Psalm 130:3-4

Carry Me

"A walk—hooray!" I always say.
My dad and I start on our way
Along the path through meadow grass
Where poppies bloom and robins play,
Walking with my dad.

But in a while I lose my smile;
My garden gate seems far away.
Tired and hot, I want to stop;
That's when I lift my arms and say,
"Carry me, Dad!"

Up so high I touch the sky
Like bumble bee and butterfly.
Safe and sound above the ground
I sit and watch the world go by,
In my daddy's arms.

God above, so full of love,
You're my Daddy God in heaven.
When I fall you hear my call
And answer to the promise given.
"Carry me, God!"

The Lord is faithful to all his promises
and loving toward all he has made.
The Lord upholds all those who fall
and lifts up all who are bowed down.

PSALM 145:13–14

Words

If I have a kind word,
A nice word,
A good word,
If I have a pleasant word
I'll speak with all my might.

But…

I Love you
you very much
help you?
you like to play?
you go first

If I have a mean word,
A bad word,
An ugly word,
If I have a naughty word
I'll zip my mouth up tight!

Set a guard over my mouth, O Lord; keep watch over
the door of my lips. —Psalm 141:3

Together

When I hear a mean word
It chases me away;
But when I hear a kind word
It makes me want to stay.

You say "Here's a cookie,"
And I say, "Have some tea."
Together we can make this world
A pleasant place to be!

How good and pleasant it is when brothers dwell together in unity. —*Psalm 133:1*

God Is Everywhere

Can God hear me in a crowd
Even though it's big and loud?

You know when I sit and when I rise; you perceive my thoughts from afar. —*Psalm 139:2*

When I'm hiding in my tree house
Just as quiet as a wee mouse,
Can God really find me there?
Yes, He can—He's everywhere!

God Is There

The heavens declare
In a voice as new
As the rising sun
And morning dew,
The heavens declare
In a voice so new—
God is there.

The heavens declare
In a voice as loud
As lightning crack
And thundercloud,
The heavens declare
In a voice so loud—
God is there.

The heavens declare the glory of God; the skies proclaim the work of his hands. —Psalm 19:1

The heavens declare in a voice as still
As moonlight streaming over the hill,
The heavens declare in a voice so still—
God is there.

He determines the number of the stars and calls them each by name. —*Psalm 147:4*

Do You Suppose

Do you suppose
The stars have names
Like Sally, Henry,
Sue, or James?
I couldn't tell—
But just the same,
God calls every star
By name!

He wraps himself in light as with a garment; he stretches

Sky Ride!

Sometimes, God puts on
His robe of shining light.
Then He steps into His chariot
(Made of clouds)
And rides with the wind
Across the sky!

out the heavens like a tent... He makes the clouds his chariot and rides on the wings of the wind. —Psalm 104:2-3

Rain

The rain comes pitter patter down
And soaks into the thirsty ground.
It makes the flowers nod hello
And helps the tender grass to grow.

He covers the sky with clouds; he supplies the earth with rain

and makes grass grow on the hills. —Psalm 147:8

He spreads the snow like

Snow

Snowflakes fall upon my house—
Quiet as a cat,
Quick as a mouse,
Down they whirl without a sound
Till they cover up the ground.

wool and scatters the frost like ashes. —Psalm 147:16

Look to the Hills

Look to the hills that reach so high,
Feet in the valley
Heads in the sky…

"Don't be afraid!"
They seem to say,
"God is watching you, night and day."

I lift up my eyes to the hills —
where does my help come from?
My help comes from the Lord,
the Maker of heaven and earth.

PSALM 121:1–2

Sing!

O sing to the Lord,
Sing a new song.
It can be short
Or it can be l – o – n – g,
quiet and soft
Or
NOISY AND STRONG
God loves them all
So sing Him a song!

Sing to the Lord a new song… —Psalm 96:1

Rejoice!

Sing, O fields and dance with glee!
Clap your hands, O forest tree!

Shout, O sky, from side to side!
Roar, you oceans deep and wide!

Every creature great and small,
Rejoice—for God is King of all!

Say among the nations, "The Lord reigns"...
Let the heavens rejoice, let the earth be glad;
let the sea resound, and all that is in it;
let the fields be jubilant, and everything in them.
Then all the trees of the forest will sing for joy;
they will sing before the Lord...

PSALM 96:10–13

Praise the Lord

BOOM ba-ba BOOM
Bangs the big bass drum.

PLAASHH…PLAASHH
Sound the cymbals.

TAH ra-ta TAH
All the trumpets shout.

TOO loo-la TOO
Cries the flute.

TAP TAP TAP
Go the dancing feet.

All of the children play and sing.
Everyone is saying the very same thing—

PRAISE THE LORD
In everything!

Praise the Lord.

Praise God in his sanctuary;
praise him in his mighty heavens.

Praise him for his acts of power;
praise him for his surpassing greatness.

Praise him with the sounding of the trumpet,
praise him with the harp and lyre,
praise him with tambourine and dancing,
praise him with the strings and flute,
praise him with the clash of cymbals....

Let everything that has breath praise the Lord.

Praise the Lord.

PSALM 150